YOU'RE INVITED TO DINNER

.... Please RSVP and attend

Rev James D Pace

ISBN 10: 1500852759
ISBN 13: 978-1500852757
Editing: E.G. Dailey

Dedication

......This book is dedicated to the loving members of

Chesed v' Shalom, who have inspired its subject matter by their love and joy during our Shabbat dinners

TABLE OF CONTENTS

FORWARD

Over the years I have watched the development of many religions, denominations and doctrines, only to see the confusion they bring to the general public. I, as a Jew and Scripture teacher, find myself and my teachings can be a part of the confusion.

However, in this book, I hope to at least mitigate and possibly remove some confusion, by taking a fresh look at some Scriptures I believe will bring many Blessings to those who read and adopt a new vision of what our God is trying to tell us. I often tell my students that *"when you read Scripture and find it confusing or in conflict with other Scripture.... take a closer look"*. In support of that statement let me emphasize that there are *no* contradictions within Scripture; I might say that if one becomes confused or doesn't understand something they read, regardless of the source, it probably needs further study. I believe that the entire Bible should be understood and followed in the manner which God intended. Often, it is the context that may be confusing, not the content.

I heard a story once, about Mark Twain (Samuel Clements) as a boy in school. On the first day of class the teacher asked "Are there any idiots in this room if so please stand up"? Of course the room fell silent. Again she asked "Are there any idiots in this room, *come now, stand up*"? Young Samuel Clements seemed to feel that the teacher was looking straight at him, but he sat silent. Once more she asked "Are there any idiots in this room"? At this point Samuel stood and looked directly at the teacher. "Samuel, do you think you are an idiot"? she asked. "No Ma'am" he replied. "Then why did you stand up" she asked. "I felt bad that you were the only one standing" Samuel replied.

Sometimes we are the only one standing; and our beliefs and convictions can make for a lonely life......but it is important that we stand regardless of others. For when we stand on truth and facts, our God stands with us......Rabbi James D Pace

INTRODUCTION

Welcome to a new way of thinking! I say a new way of thinking, but I really should say 'A new way to look at Scripture'. This new way is not frightening, weird or cultic, and should not be construed as an attempt of changing or converting your core beliefs. But I am going to challenge you by asking this question: Would you like to experience the joy of having a Blessing of God you haven't had the opportunity to experience before? If your answer is yes, then let's start our exciting journey.

There are some things we need to bring to mind before proceeding; these *may* sound controversial, at first, but they really aren't. I'll ask you to face them with an open mind, and most importantly, an open heart, so that our quest for Blessings filled with Joy can be a real experience.

Here are the new concepts to consider:

1. The bulk (majority) of the Bible is the story about the Jewish people and Israel, not the Gentile or pagan world.

2. The Scriptures are clear – through Abraham's descendants (the Jewish people) the Nations of the World will be blessed.
3. The Scriptures were written down by Jewish men, who received their inspiration from the Holy Spirit of God, and it is through Jewish eyes that we must *first* look, in order to obtain the *context* of the Scripture. Once the context is understood, we can analyze the content and apply the results to our personal lives. (Text without context is pretext ….author unknown)
4. God is the creator of all humans, including those of Jewish, Christian, Pagan or whatever background you choose to cite; and that same God loves each of his creations – even if they choose to walk in ways that are not pleasing to Him.
5. Even though God commands the Jewish people to live a certain way, adhering to the commands of life found in the Torah (The first five books of the Bible; the Books of Moses), He invites the rest of the world (all people) to join with Israel and those observant Jewish people, in a lifestyle that

is not only pleasing to our God, but can be healthier and happier than we may have been experiencing.

Throughout what we call The Old Testament, we find references to some special times that God insists the people observe. These are called "God's appointed times" (in Hebrew Moadim). Some things that pop out when first reading these Scriptures are that: These times are special to God, are commanded of the Jewish people, include a meal and are to be a 'holy convocation'. That last one, 'holy convocation' is often misunderstood.

> **Holy**: In this case, the word holy does not mean pious or some arrogant moral status that seems unattainable, but simply means different or set apart.

> **Convocation:** To me, when I hear the word 'convocation' I immediately think of the graduation ceremony where my son, Zach, received his Masters Degree. The time was filled with speeches, music, pageantry and caps and gowns; it was a very special event filled with much joy. In the Biblical context,

and for our purposes, a 'convocation' is a special occasion that may be augmented by the foregoing descriptive words, but for sure it is to be an event that is different from any other gathering; one where the invitation comes from our God, and asks us to join Him in some sort of celebration.

Therefore, a Holy Convocation is a celebration that is, and should be, unlike any other celebration we might attend. It should be so different, that it stands apart from any birthday party, wedding banquet, graduation ceremony, barbecue or football tailgate party we might be invited to, or organize. Additionally, our expectations, attitudes and excitement should be greater than those mustered up by other happy and fun occasions.

Are you still with me? OK, let's take a look at some Scripture: Most translations of the Bible will work fine, but I prefer the New American Standard Bible (NASB) and will be using that translation for most of our adventure.

In the Bible, as mentioned before, there are several citations regarding God's appointed times. Those times when He has called His people into a

Holy Convocation at which He is present. Why not? He's the one who invited us to the event. Of all the citations, Leviticus 23 seems to have the most complete list of those times.

Leviticus 23 (NASB*): ¹The LORD spoke again to Moses, saying, ²"Speak to the sons of Israel and say to them, 'The LORD'S appointed times which you shall proclaim as holy convocations—My appointed times are these:*

SABBATH

³'For six days work may be done, but on the seventh day there is a Sabbath of complete rest, a holy convocation. You shall not do any work; it is a Sabbath to the LORD in all your dwellings.

PASSOVER

⁴'These are the appointed times of the LORD, holy convocations which you shall proclaim at the times appointed for them. ⁵'In the first month, on the fourteenth day of the month at twilight is the LORD'S Passover.

UNLEAVENED BREAD

⁶'Then on the fifteenth day of the same month there is the Feast of Unleavened Bread to the LORD; for seven days you shall eat unleavened bread. ⁷'On the first day you shall have a holy convocation; you shall not do any laborious work. ⁸'But for seven days you shall present an offering by fire to the LORD. On the seventh day is a holy convocation; you shall not do any laborious work.'"

SHAVUOT (PENTECOST)

⁹Then the LORD spoke to Moses, saying, ¹⁰"Speak to the sons of Israel and say to them, 'When you enter the land which I am going to give to you and reap its harvest, then you shall bring in the sheaf of the first fruits of your harvest to the priest. ¹¹'He shall wave the sheaf before the LORD for you to be accepted; on the day after the Sabbath the priest shall wave it. ¹²'Now on the day when you wave the sheaf, you shall offer a male lamb one-year-old without defect for a burnt offering to the LORD. ¹³'Its grain offering shall then be two-tenths of an ephah of fine flour mixed with oil, an offering by fire to the LORD for a soothing aroma, with its drink offering, a fourth of a £hin of wine. ¹⁴'Until this same day, until you have brought in the offering of your God, you shall eat neither bread nor roasted grain nor new growth. It is to be a perpetual statute throughout your generations in all your dwelling places.

¹⁵'You shall also count for yourselves from the day after the Sabbath, from the day when you brought in the sheaf of the wave offering; there shall be seven complete sabbaths. ¹⁶'You shall count fifty days to the day after the seventh sabbath; then you shall present a new grain offering to the LORD. ¹⁷'You shall bring in from your dwelling places two loaves of bread for a wave offering, made of two-tenths of an ephah; they shall be of a fine flour, baked with leaven as first fruits to the LORD. ¹⁸'Along with the bread you shall present seven one year old male lambs without defect, and a bull of the herd and two rams; they are to be a burnt offering to the LORD, with their grain offering and their drink offerings, an offering by fire of a soothing aroma to the LORD. ¹⁹'You shall also offer one male goat for a sin offering and two male lambs one year old for a sacrifice of peace offerings. ²⁰'The priest shall then wave them with the bread of the first fruits for a wave offering with two lambs before the LORD; they are to be holy to the Lord for the priest. ²¹'On this same day you shall make a proclamation as well; you are to have a holy convocation. You shall do no laborious work. It is to be a perpetual statute in all your dwelling places throughout your generations.

²²'When you reap the harvest of your land, moreover, you shall not reap to the very corners of your field nor gather the gleaning of your harvest; you are to leave them for the needy and the alien. I am the LORD your God.'"

ROSH HASHANAH

²³Again the LORD spoke to Moses, saying, ²⁴"Speak to the sons of Israel, saying, 'In the seventh month on the first of the month you shall have a rest, a reminder by blowing of trumpets, a holy convocation. ²⁵'You shall not do any laborious work, but you shall present an offering by fire to the LORD.'

DAY OF ATONEMENT

26The LORD spoke to Moses, saying, 27"On exactly the tenth day of this seventh month is the day of atonement; it shall be a holy convocation for you, and you shall humble your souls and present an offering by fire to the LORD. 28"You shall not do any work on this same day, for it is a day of atonement, to make atonement on your behalf before the LORD your God. 29"If there is any person who will not humble himself on this same day, he shall be cut off from his people. 30"As for any person who does any work on this same day, that person I will destroy from among his people. 31"You shall do no work at all. It is to be a perpetual statute throughout your generations in all your dwelling places. 32"It is to be a sabbath of complete rest to you, and you shall humble your souls; on the ninth of the month at evening, from evening until evening you shall keep your sabbath."

FEAST OF BOOTHS

33Again the LORD spoke to Moses, saying, 34"Speak to the sons of Israel, saying, 'On the fifteenth of this seventh month is the Feast of

Booths for seven days to the LORD. ³⁵'On the first day is a holy convocation; you shall do no laborious work of any kind. ³⁶'For seven days you shall present an offering by fire to the LORD. On the eighth day you shall have a holy convocation and present an offering by fire to the LORD; it is an assembly. You shall do no laborious work.

³⁷'These are the appointed times of the LORD which you shall proclaim as holy convocations, to present offerings by fire to the LORD—burnt offerings and grain offerings, sacrifices and drink offerings, each day's matter on its own day— ³⁸besides those of the Sabbaths of the LORD, and besides your gifts and besides all your votive and freewill offerings, which you give to the LORD.

³⁹'On exactly the fifteenth day of the seventh month, when you have gathered in the crops of the land, you shall celebrate the feast of the LORD for seven days, with a rest on the first day and a rest on the eighth day. ⁴⁰'Now on the first day you shall take for yourselves the foliage of beautiful trees, palm branches and boughs of leafy trees and willows of the brook, and you shall rejoice before the LORD your God for seven

days. ⁴¹'You shall thus celebrate it as a feast to the LORD for seven days in the year. It shall be a perpetual statute throughout your generations; you shall celebrate it in the seventh month. ⁴²'You shall live in booths for seven days; all the native-born in Israel shall live in booths, ⁴³so that your generations may know that I had the sons of Israel live in booths when I brought them out from the land of Egypt. I am the LORD your God.' ⁴⁴So Moses declared to the sons of Israel the appointed times of the LORD.

Well, there we are; the core Scripture for our new look at God's appointed times. Look at the last verse "So Moses declared to the sons of Israel the appointed times of the Lord"; not man's appointed times or church appointed times, but *appointed times of the Lord!* Let me say here that there are a lot of man's appointed times and a lot of church appointed times, and that's OK. I'm just as much into tradition as the next person, but for now and this new adventure into Blessings and joy, we are only dealing with those times that God has established. I will, at later points in this book, discuss some of man's appointed or declared times.

The 23rd Chapter of Leviticus needs a little context. I'll deal with the first context here and other aspects in later chapters. First, what are those appointed times of God that He commands Israel to observe and invites all others to join in? They are:

- The Passover and Feast of Unleavened Bread
- Shavuot or the Feast of Weeks (Pentecost)
- Yom Turah or Rosh Hashanah
- Yom Kippur or Day of Atonement
- Succoth or Feast of Booths (Tabernacles)
- Shabbat or Sabbath

Each of the appointed times of God are, in His Words, *Holy Convocations*. And each of the appointed times is to be a joyous occasion with prayer, ritual and celebrating. Each event has associated with it a special meal: good food, good drink and good fellowship. Each celebration has the same host, the one true God of the Universe. He has established these special anointed times to gather with those who proclaim Him to be God. It is at these special times in which we can find special blessings of joy; this can only come from Him. And it is these special occasions that we *all*

are invited to, each year. There it is: You're
invited to Dinner, over 60 times a year, and the
invitation comes from your God!

Chapter 1: Sacrifices, Burnt Offerings, Drink Offerings, Grain Offerings???

In traditional Christian teachings, any time the word 'sacrifice' or the description of any ancient offerings are mentioned, some people get immediately turned off. The thoughts of a bloody mess of animal carcasses and constant fires burning animals into heaps of ashes, conjures up mental images that the modern person cannot abide.

I was visiting the ancient ruins of Petra in Jordan, one day, listening to my guide explain some of the ruins of the Nabataean society that once occupied the beautiful surroundings. He kept referring to sacrifices of the people and the high places where they would have those sacrifices. I finally asked him what he thought a sacrifice was. He quickly responded "a meal that was dedicated to a specific god by the incantation of a prayer". I was stunned and relieved at the same time. Finally, he gave an answer that not only made sense, but described every meal that I had ever prayed over as a sacrifice.

Finally, a sacrifice was nothing to be afraid of or run away from. Now it all made sense because *now* I had some important context to apply to the understanding of this Scripture. Celebrating the appointed times of God with a meal, is a sacrifice!

Additionally, one of the important words to translate here (Leviticus 23) is the Hebrew word Aw-saw (transliterated) which can mean to *make ready to observe*. It is the word that we sometimes translate into 'sacrifice'. So for us, our 'sacrifice' is something that we make ready for our observance; *a meal to partake of during our Holy Convocation.*

Again, you see, the sacrifice that we offer in our *context* is not a bad thing; it is a pleasing meal that may include: meat (I prefer lamb), grains (I prefer bread especially cornbread) and various drinks (alcoholic or nonalcoholic). We then garnish our meal with various vegetables (again my preferences....asparagus and potatoes), which are to please the taste buds and bring forth happiness and joy, all in the presence of our God.

Confusing? Maybe. Why did we get the wrong impression of what a sacrifice was? Because of various translators and commentators and the fact that there are some sacrifices that are not eaten as a meal; but that is a subject for another book.

So for our purposes and the context of Leviticus 23:

- Burnt offering – meat
- Grain offering – bread
- Drink offering – it could be Snapple©
- Sacrifice – a great meal shared with fellow believers and our God

Chapter 2: You're invited to Dinner

I like to go out to dinner. It's not something I do very often because of the cost of a good restaurant; but I still like going, especially when going out with a group of people for a special occasion. I suppose this goes back to my growing up years, as my family looked for opportunities to get together for a good meal and celebration. We would actually look for reasons to celebrate.....such as *Tuesday*. At one point my mom took a cue from Alice in Wonderland, and we began celebrating our 'unbirthdays'. When we got together, it was always exciting and fun. Even when my brothers and I had our own families, getting together was very special. The anticipation, the excitement, the laughing and of course the meal was an expression of the love we had for each other and for the family unit. Sadly, upon the death of our mother, the traditional gatherings became fewer and far between, although there are discussions at times of getting together – and when we do, it is joyful and certainly brings back great memories.

It is the same sort of anticipation, excitement and joy that I want to instill in you, as you begin to understand the appointed times of our God. As we prepare to come together with one another and meet with our God over a 'sacrifice' of a meal and celebration (see the word sacrifice didn't sound that bad now, did it?), let us do so with the same or even greater excitement and anticipation that would accompany us when we get ready for a meal or celebration of other events.

What stops us from the celebration of God's appointed times? Well there is a Scripture often quoted that, unfortunately, is misunderstood: **Romans 14:5 et seq -** *[5] One person regards one day above another, another regards every day alike. Each person must be fully convinced in his own mind. [6] He who observes the day, observes it for the Lord, and he who eats, does so for the Lord, for he gives thanks to God; and he who eats not, for the Lord he does not eat, and gives thanks to God. [7] For not one of us lives for himself, and not one dies for himself; [8] for if we live, we live for the Lord, or if we die, we* *die for the Lord; therefore whether we live or die, we are the Lord's. [9] For to this end Christ died and lived again, that He might be Lord both of the dead and of the living.*

At first reading of these verses, we might get the impression there are no special days, foods or events in the architecture of our God; however that is because this set of Scriptures is read without the benefit of verses that directly precede verse 5 or the context in which they were written.

Let's begin by looking at context:

> First of all, the Book of Romans was written to a collection of Jews and Gentiles, living in Rome, who believed that Jesus (Yeshua) was the Messiah. It is important to understand that at that time, (between 56 and 57 AD) Christianity had not fully developed to the point where it was recognized as separate from Judaism. At that time (and the time that the Book of Romans is talking about) Christians were merely a division/sect of Judaism.

Second, the Roman community of believers lived in a most important pagan city of the times that was filled with pagan rituals, beliefs and special days.

Finally, the Apostle Paul was concerned for the believers and their relationships toward their pagan neighbors, who potentially could become believers – as long as the believing community exampled the truth through the 'love of God', *which prohibited judgment of others and of their special days and practices.*

We need to remember that Paul was a believing Jew, who through his own testimony in the courts of Rome, never rejected his Jewish beliefs or practices. *So why would we think in this case, he would proclaim that God's appointed times had no place in the lives of the Roman believers?* He didn't!

Now that we have established some context, let's look at Romans 14 verses 1 to 4: **Now accept the one who is weak in faith, but not for the purpose of passing judgment on his opinions. ² One person has faith that he may eat all things, but he who** *is weak eats vegetables only. ³ The one who eats is not to regard with contempt the one who does not eat, and the one who does not eat is not to judge the one who eats, for God has accepted him. ⁴ Who are you to judge the servant of another? To his own master he stands or falls; and he will stand, for the Lord is able to make him stand.*

"Accept the one who is weak in faith, but not for the purpose of passing judgment on his opinions"? Indeed, the Apostle is giving us a rule that should apply to us today as well as to those in Rome, in those days. The key words are "weak in faith" – this is not referring to Jews of the time, who observed special days, or even the Messianic Congregations of today. It is referring *only* to the pagan residents of Rome who certainly were 'weak in faith'.   As the Apostle is teaching, he says 'don't judge them'. It is hard not to agree with Paul, when you see the context of his letter. Frankly I don't know of anyone who was ever 'judged' into the Kingdom; or found the Messiah and the love of God because their neighbor judged them for their beliefs.

Now, back to my question: What hinders us from celebrating God's appointed times? We stop ourselves because we have been taught wrong for centuries. Certainly our God doesn't stop or prohibit us! You see, God did not invite us to dinner in one part of His book, and then later tell us He wasn't interested in having dinner with us.

Yes, we have been invited to dinner with our God. And as He looks forward to that event, we need to RSVP and then attend. So let's do it! Let's get excited and happy that we have a loving God, who established special days/events, and wishes to meet with us on those special days. Yes indeed, He will meet us every day, but God established *'special days'* for us. Isn't that great?

Chapter 3: Shabbat

Now that you have been invited to dinner, you need to RSVP, but first we need to know when and where the dinner will be held.

The where is very interesting, inasmuch as not all of the invitations are for the same location, Biblically speaking, that is. So let's take the invitations one at a time and mark our calendars together.

Shabbat (Sabbath): In Exodus we begin to see a pattern developing as the whole congregation of Israel begins to complain about not having enough to eat. They complained to Moses and Aaron saying that in Egypt, even though they were slaves, their pots were full. But now they questioned why they were out there in the desert barely surviving. Eventually, the wailing and complaining is temporarily put on hold, as God provides both meat and bread to fill their stomachs and remove the hunger pangs.

I can't imagine a meal of 'all you can eat' quail and bread. I'm sure it had some desert greens and wine, possibly some goat cheese, but in the end they were filled and satisfied.

Next, in Exodus 16 beginning at verse 21, we see our first invitation to dinner which includes the time and place. I will say that the time is much clearer than the place.

²²Now on the sixth day they gathered twice as much bread, two omers for each one. When all the leaders of the congregation came and told Moses, ²³then he said to them, "This is what the LORD meant: Tomorrow is a sabbath observance, a holy sabbath to the LORD. Bake what you will bake and boil what you will boil, and all that is left over put aside to be kept until morning." ²⁴So they put it aside until morning, as Moses had ordered, and it did not become foul nor was there any worm in it. ²⁵Moses said, "Eat it today, for today is a sabbath to the LORD; today you will not find it in the field. ²⁶"Six days you shall gather it, but on the seventh day, the Sabbath, there will be none."

²⁷It came about on the seventh day that some of the people went out to gather, but they found none. ²⁸Then the LORD said to Moses, "How long *do you refuse to keep My commandments and My instructions? ²⁹"See, the LORD has given you the Sabbath; therefore He gives you bread for two days on the sixth day. Remain every man in his place; let no man go out of his place on the seventh day." ³⁰So the people rested on the seventh day.*

³¹The house of Israel named it manna, and it was like coriander seed, white, and its taste was like wafers with honey. ³²Then Moses said, "This is what the LORD has commanded, 'Let an omerful of it be kept throughout your generations, that they may see the bread that I fed you in the wilderness, when I brought you out of the land of Egypt.'" ³³Moses said to Aaron, "Take a jar and put an omer full of manna in it, and place it before the LORD to be kept throughout your generations." ³⁴As the LORD commanded Moses, so Aaron placed it before the Testimony, to be kept. ³⁵The sons of Israel ate the manna forty years, until they came to an inhabited land; they ate the manna until they came to the border of the land of Canaan.

There it is, the time for the first dinner invitation was in fact one of God's appointed times, the Shabbat (Sabbath). When? It is every 7 days and begins at sundown, when the sixth day ends and continues to sundown of the seventh day. During that time, we are to eat and rest! The *where* is pointed out in verse 29: **Remain every man in his place; let no man go out of his place on the seventh day. [30]So the people rested on the seventh day.** At that time, there were no places for corporate worship, so it made sense for people to have this special dinner in their homes, with their families.

Our next citation can be found in Exodus 20 beginning at verse 8: **Remember the Sabbath and keep it holy.** Once again we see that our God declares that the Sabbath needs to be quite different than any other day of the week and therefore the meal that goes along with the Sabbath needs to be different than any other meal of the week.

But how do we RSVP? Simple, make a commitment to attend Shabbat dinner each week.

I'll talk about how dinner might be prepared and observed in a latter chapter.

So we have the time and place; always on Sabbath and where our family takes a meal. Certainly at first reading we can see that the Sabbath meal should be in the home (**let no man go out of his place**) however, over time we have been gathering for a Sabbath meal in some of our Synagogues and other places of worship, to share a meal with like believers. In Deuteronomy 14:26 we see the command of God to eat our offerings in the presence of the Lord, in a place where He places His name. Surely God places His name on our houses of worship, as well as our homes; therefore, having a sacrificial meal in either place is not a problem; or in our home or the home of another believer where God's holy name is revered. The point to be made here is that on every Sabbath we are invited to eat a meal with like believers and in the presence of our God.

Who is invited to these 52 Sabbath dinners*?*
Exodus 23:12 says: [12] *"Six days you are to do your work, but on the seventh day you shall cease from labor so that your ox and your donkey may*

rest, and the son of your female slave, as well as your stranger, may refresh themselves."

So for the appointed time of Sabbath, *the invitation to dinner is every week on the seventh day and everyone is invited; even you.* How will you respond? Will you RSVP - tell God you are accepting His invitation to Shabbat dinner?

Chapter 4: Rosh Hashanah

We have taken care of the *weekly* invitation, but what about the various invitations that come once a year; *Passover, Feast of Weeks, Rosh Hashanah, Yom Kippur and Feast of Booths?*

Rosh Hashanah: Just before Yom Kippur is a celebration time that goes by different names; it is what has been labeled the *Jewish New Year* or Rosh Hashanah. There may be some confusion about the 'New Year' because of the traditional December 31-January 1 celebration in secular society, and the four special New Year beginnings in Jewish custom.

> 1st of Nisan: The first New Year is the 1st of the Hebrew month of Nisan, usually in the early spring. The 1st of Nisan was considered the New Year for counting the years of the reigns of kings in ancient Israel. It is also the New Year for ordering the Jewish holidays. The month of Nisan is closely tied with the festival of Passover, while Rosh Hashanah is seen as the anniversary of the creation of the world, the 1st of Nisan is seen in a way as the

anniversary of the founding of the Jewish people when they escaped from Egypt during the Passover story.

1st of Elul: The second "new year" is on the 1st of Elul, the sixth month of the Hebrew calendar which usually falls in the late summer. According to the Mishnah this was the New Year for animal tithes. It was used to determine the start date for the animal tithe to the priestly class in ancient Israel, similar to how we use April 15th in the US as tax day. Generally this New Year is no longer observed, although the month of Elul does mark the beginning of preparations for Rosh Hashanah.

1st of Tishrei, aka Rosh Hashanah: Rosh Hashanah is the Jewish New Year we are most familiar with. It falls on the 1st of Tishrei, the seventh month of the Hebrew calendar, which usually corresponds to sometime in the month of September. It marks the day when the Jewish calendar year advances and is seen traditionally as the date when the world was created.

15th of Shvat, aka Tu B'Shvat: Tu B'Shvat is considered the New Year for trees, usually falling between January and February. According to the Torah fruits cannot be consumed from trees less than three years old, Tu B'Shvat was used as the starting date for determining the age of the trees. Unlike the 1st of Nisan and the 1st of Elul, Tu B'Shvat is still widely observed as a minor Jewish holiday.

That all being said, although there is no prohibition in Jewish or Christian practices that speak against New Year and other celebrations established by man unless they are truly pagan wherein a pagan god is celebrated, participation can be fun. Rosh Hashanah, however, is one of the appointed times of our God. So, let's explore it and accept the invitation.

The name "Rosh Hashanah" (head of the year) is not used in Scripture to describe this appointed time; the verses found in Leviticus 23, refer to the holiday as Yom Ha-Zikkaron (Transliterated yoam-zeek-are-oan) – which is the day of remembrance or Yom Teruah (Transliterated yoam-tay-roo-ah) –

which means the day of the sounding of the shofar/day of blowing.

A popular observance during this holiday is eating apples dipped in honey, a symbol of our wish for a sweet new year. There are congregational gatherings, the multiple blowing of the shofar, meals, music, dancing and of course the traditional greeting - L'Shanah Tovah (transliterated li-shah-nah toe-vah) which means 'have a good year' year' or Chag Sameach (transliterated hawg-sa-may-ack), which wishes one a 'joyous festival'.

Styles of celebration vary from community to community, but all in all it is a wonderful celebration of anticipation of the sweet and prosperous New Year, celebrating with friends and family and of course doing so in the presence of our God.

We know the when, but what about the where? Well, we need to be good 'Bible Detectives' to find out the where.

23 Again the Lord spoke to Moses, saying, 24 "Speak to the sons of Israel, saying, 'In

the seventh month on the first of the month you shall have a rest, a reminder by blowing of trumpets, a holy convocation. [25] You shall not do any laborious work, but you shall present an offering by fire to the Lord." (Leviticus 23:23-25)

As you can see in the Scripture, which institutes this Appointed Time, there is no actual place cited. However, we see that it is Moses speaking to the sons of Israel and we know they are all together before the Mishkan (Tent of Meeting). Thus the place for celebration is in a *congregational* setting. For our purposes, this could be at any site you choose, where people could assemble. We celebrate at synagogue, with liturgy, shofar blowing and a great meal – accented with apples and honey.

Chapter 5: Yom Kippur

Yom Kippur (the Day of Atonement): Again, the when and where are the questions to ask of our invitation to dinner.

Leviticus 23:27 gives us the when*: ²⁶The LORD spoke to Moses, saying, ²⁷"On exactly the tenth day of this seventh month is the day of atonement; it shall be a holy convocation for you, and you shall humble your souls and present an offering by fire to the LORD."* When is the seventh month of the year? Well on the modern calendar it is the month of July. However, we are back to that word 'context' and in context the seventh month being addressed here is the seventh month of the Hebrew calendar which is the month of Tishrei (Transliterated tish-ree). So each year in the seventh month on the tenth day, we are invited to another holy convocation.

This holy convocation is quite different from all the rest. It has been called the "most holy day of the Jewish calendar". Now we know when.....let's look at where this event is to take place.

Leviticus 23:31 gives us two important clues as to how important this appointed time is: *³¹"You shall do no work at all. It is to be a perpetual statute throughout your generations in all your dwelling places."* As we search for the where, we have a wonderful opportunity to find out how long this yearly meeting with our God should be. The word 'perpetual' is translated from the Hebrew word that is (transliterated o-lawm), which means 'forever' or 'never stopping'. Other translations will say 'in every generation' or some phrase that will connote a long period of time. So we know the time, and we know that this convocation needs to continue each year forever; now the place.

"In all your dwelling places", says the Scripture. At first glance we might consider the reference to our houses or tents, but again we need a little context. From the Hebrew word (transliterated mo-shawb), we have the definition of a seat (like a County seat) or place, where a population dwells. There are other definitions, but for our purposes we will use this one and our mo-shawb is our community, which seems to be how the Sages

looked at the word and established the traditions of Synagogue assembly for the Day of Atonement.

On this holy day, we don't actually have a meal, as from sundown to sundown we participate in a complete fast. We do however celebrate! For this is a time to bring the sins of the past year before our God, and rejoice in the fact that He forgives those sins, when we are honest about our resolve to make things right and attempt not to repeat them. There is so much more that happens on Yom Kippur in the way of liturgy and actions, *but what about that invitation to dinner?*

After the twenty fifth hour of the fast (we add an hour to this one) the shofar is blown and the fast ends with a celebratory meal, as we celebrate the forgiving of our sins and the brightness of a new year with a chance to make our lives and the lives of others, better. This sacrificial meal can take place at home, at congregation or some even go to a restaurant and celebrate publicly.

Chapter 6: Feast of Tabernacles

Feast of Tabernacles: Five days after Yom Kippur, we get another invitation to dinner; actually seven dinners. The first is the first day of the Feast of Tabernacles or Feast of Booths; in Hebrew Sukkot or Succoth (transliterated sue-kote).

The time is set as the fifteenth day of the seventh month (every year) and the place is 'in booths' or temporary dwellings. This celebration is pretty simple; it takes place out of the normal house and lasts for seven days. The booths are decorated with vegetables, fruits and greenery, from the Fall harvest. Some congregations actually build a booth and participate in some liturgy while in the booth, but each family should have their own booth and take their meals in it.

Here in the Pacific Northwest we often contend with weather that is not conducive to living in the booth for seven days, but we do make an attempt to obey the commandment. This celebration is not only a reminder of the time the Israelites spent in the desert, but also a time to celebrate the plenty of the harvest. It is from this tradition that modern societies developed the institution of Thanksgiving Day, an annual modern feast.

It is in the description of the feasts that we finally get a good understanding of the sacrifices that are offered at each celebration. **Leviticus 23:37** [37] ***"These are the appointed times of the LORD which you shall proclaim as holy convocations, to present offerings by fire to the LORD—burnt offerings and grain offerings, sacrifices and drink offerings, each day's matter on its own day"*** Those offerings are the meals that we eat in the presence of our God. They are His gifts to us, and our being there at the meal is our gift of obedience to Him. In these verses the word gift is translated from a Hebrew word that is pronounced **maw-taw-naw**, which in a good sense means a special gift or sacrificial offering. But as in all languages we must be careful in the use of this particular word, because it can also mean, in a bad sense, a bribe. Clearly we are not trying to bribe God, nor is He trying to bribe us.....so we will translate this word to mean *a special and good gift.*

So, we have Shabbat, Rosh Hashanah, Yom Kippur, Feast of Booths....what other initiations do we have? Well there are a couple of appointed times left. Let's keep learning!

Chapter 7: Passover

Passover: Pesach (transliterated pay-sock) or Passover is a holiday that comes in the springtime when the earth is becoming green with life. It is a celebration where we observe some of the same ancient traditions of the sons of Israel, as they anticipated their departure from Egypt.

The Passover is the longest continuing religious observance in world history. In Jewish homes, Passover is a special time of preparation, celebration and reflection on the wonderful things that our God has done. What a great opportunity to enjoy the company of family and friends as we teach, celebrate and enjoy a wonderful dinner, in the presence of our God.

The Passover Seder tells a story of God's mighty deliverance of the children of Israel from their bondage in Egypt. Rich in symbolism, this festival is a tapestry of sounds, sights and smells that enhance the celebration and gives us a shadow of what was and will be.

"In the first month, on the fourteenth day of the month at twilight is the Lord's Passover. (Leviticus 23:5) It is a night to be observed for the Lord for having brought them out from the land of Egypt; this night is for the Lord, to be observed by all the sons of Israel throughout their generations." (Exodus 12:42)

And other Scriptures tell us what, how to eat and where. We eat unleavened breads, but since the second temple was destroyed in 70 AD, lamb is no longer eaten at the Passover. Beef, chicken or other kosher meats replace the lamb.

So the time is set, the place is in our homes and the meal, well it is filled with wonderful meat, good drink, fresh herbs and vegetables. The Scripture also says that we should share our meal; because of that teaching, we invite as many people as we can. *[4] "Now if the household is too small for a lamb, then he and his neighbor nearest to his house are to take one according to the number of persons in them; according to what each man should eat, you are to divide the lamb" (Exodus 12:4)*

Finally, the Passover requires the telling of the Exodus story. *²⁶ **And when your children say to you, 'What does this rite mean to you?' ²⁷ you shall say, 'It is a Passover sacrifice to the Lord who passed over the houses of the sons of Israel in Egypt when He smote the Egyptians, but spared our homes.' And the people bowed low and worshiped. (Exodus 12:26)***

The Passover Seder is pretty well scripted, so if you have never participated in one, you can buy a script or small book called a Haggadah (transliterated hawg-ah-dah). One good one is Celebrate Passover ©, by James D Pace…. oh, that's me! By the way, that little 'c' after the title is a copyright symbol. Please don't photocopy, just get one for everyone at the Seder. There are other books printed with many different traditions and orders of the meal.

Chapter 8: Feast of Weeks

Shavuot: Shavuot (Transliterated shaw-voo-ote) the Feast of Weeks – known in Christian circles as Pentecost - is the second of the three major festivals with both historical and agricultural significance, the other two being Passover and Sukkoth.

Agriculturally, Shavuot commemorates the time when the first fruits were harvested and brought to the Temple, and is known as Hag ha-Bikkurim, the Festival of the First Fruits, (Transliterated Hawg-beek-oo-reem). Historically, it celebrates the giving of the Torah, the Word of God, at Mount Sinai.

"You shall count for yourselves -- from the day after the Shabbat, from the day when you bring the Omer of the waving -- seven Shabbats, they shall be complete. Until the day after the seventh sabbath you shall count, fifty days... You shall convoke on this very day -- there shall be a holy convocation for yourselves -- you shall do no laborious work; it is an eternal decree in your dwelling places for your generations." Leviticus 23:15-16, 21

Shavuot is not tied to a particular calendar date. Instead the Festival is connected to a counting of days and weeks from Passover. Because the length of the months used to be variable, determined by observation, and there are two new moons between Passover and Shavuot, the beginning of the Festival could occur on the 5th or 6th of Sivan. However, now that we have a mathematically determined calendar, and the months between Passover and Shavuot do not change length on the mathematical calendar, the Festival is always on the 6th of Sivan (the 6th and 7th outside of Israel.

There has been much discussion among the sages about the beginning of the Festival, along with some disagreement. However, all sources agree on one thing: *There must be a Festival!*

Shavuot dinner is great, because dairy products are the meal of the day. *Oh darn, do you mean I have to eat ice cream and cheesecake?* It's too bad this Festival isn't longer.

There are a few opinions as to why dairy dishes are preferred. Some say it is a reminder of the promise regarding the land of Israel, a land flowing with "milk and honey." According to others, it is because our ancestors had just received the Torah (and the dietary laws therein), and did not have both meat and dairy dishes available.   Regardless of the reason, it is a great celebration and the food is wonderful.

So there you go. The appointed times of our God. Times that He has set aside for special dinners that you are invited to and He will host. These times are special, fun, educational and spiritual. It is a shame that more people don't experience the blessings that come with these celebrations. Why don't you give them a try? I think you will be surprised how wonderful they can be.

Chapter 9: Written Invitations

You Are Invited to Shabbat Dinner

When: Every Friday Evening at Sundown

Where: In Your Home with Family and Friends

Meal to be served: Delicious Meat, Vegetables, Breads and Desserts

Please R.S.V.P.

The Shabbat dinner is accented with two candles and wonderful Challah (transliterated hall-ah), a very tasty braided bread. By the way, Challah makes great French toast!

Shabbat dinner is truly a familial event. Moms, dads, and children, make for a great evening of food, song, laughter and very special blessings said over the evening, moms and the children, by the head of the household. The attempt is to make the meal the most special meal of the week. Dressing up and dinner by candlelight; how could it get any better?

> ### *You Are Invited to Succoth Dinner*
>
> When: At sundown on the 15th day of of the Hebrew Month Tishrei
>
> Where: In a temporary booth, with Family and Friends
>
> Meal to be served: Fresh vegetables, fruits and grains that represent the Autumn harvest, are the fare de jur.
>
> Please R.S.V.P.

The holiday lasts seven days in Israel and eight in the diaspora. The first day (and second day in the diaspora) is a Shabbat-like holiday when work is forbidden. The festival is closed with another Shabbat-like holiday called Shemini Atzeret (two days in the diaspora, where the second day is called Simchat Torah).

A break-fast is a delicious and celebratory meal eaten after Jewish fast days such as Yom Kippur and Tisha B'Av. During a Jewish fast, no food or drink is consumed, including bread and water, so the meal is usually one 'of plenty'. The Yom Kippur fasts last over 25 hours, from before sundown on the previous night until after sundown on the day of the fast. I always stop here and remind people that our God is not foolish. If you are unable to fast for medical reasons DON'T! Take your physician prescribed medications; God would rather you survive and celebrate.

> ### *You Are Invited to Rosh Hashanah Dinner*
>
> When: After sundown on the 1rst day of the Hebrew
> month of Tishrei
>
> Where: Anywhere with Family and Friends
>
> Meal to be Served: Delicious Meat, Vegetables, Breads
> and Desserts all accented with apples and honey
>
> Please R.S.V.P.

We generally fix a very huge dinner with a large roast or brisket, plenty of vegetables, fresh greens and of course plenty of desserts. The evening is marked with toasts wishing one another a sweet new year, generally using apples dipped in honey.

You Are Invited to Shavuot Dinner

When: 50 days following Passover

Where: In Your Home with Family and Friends

Meal to be Served: Delicious Meat, Vegetables, Breads and Desserts

Please R.S.V.P.

This meal is accented with dairy products; milk, cheeses, ice cream and of course Cheesecake.

You Are Invited to Passover Dinner

When: The evening of the 14th day of the

Hebrew month Nisan

Where: In Your Home with Family and

Friends

Meal to be Served: Delicious Meat,

Vegetables, Breads and Desserts

Please R.S.V.P.

This is a very special meal, where family and friends gather to re-tell the story of the Passover and the Exodus from Egypt. Although the menu varies from region to region, it is accented by the use of Matzo instead of other bread products. Having a great meal is important, but the key point of the evening is the story of our God's redemption power.

Chapter 10: Can We Invite God to Our Special Dinners?

I know there are some still reading who are asking "can we invite God to our special events". The answer is, *indeed you can and should!*

I certainly believe God needs to be present in all of our celebrations: daily meals, birthdays, anniversaries, graduations, retirements etc.; any time we get together over a meal, we should do so in the presence of our God. Meals and prayer are pretty traditional in most religious circles, but here's a thought – why not say a prayer at the end of your meal, instead of the traditional beginning…..actually you can do both, but did you know the after meal prayer is a command of God?

[10] " When you have eaten and are satisfied, you shall bless the Lord your God for the good land which He has given you." (Deuteronomy 8:10)

Remembering special events and times that we humans have instituted is OK too. In fact, I encourage it. Even in Jewish tradition there are several established times that are not God initiated but man initiated; great times for a celebration with good food and good company.

Feast of Esther: Purim (Transliterated pur-eem) is known as the Feast of Esther. *"**In the twelfth month, which is the month of Adar, on its thirteenth day ... on the day that the enemies of the Jews were expected to prevail over them, it was turned about: The Jews prevailed over their adversaries. (Esther 9:1) ²⁰ Then Mordecai recorded these events, and he sent letters to all the Jews who were in all the provinces of King Ahasuerus, both near and far, ²¹ obliging them to celebrate the fourteenth day of the month Adar, and the fifteenth day of the same month, annually,²² because on those days the Jews [l]rid themselves of their enemies, and it was a month which was turned for them from sorrow into gladness and from mourning into a holiday; that they should make them days of feasting and rejoicing and sending portions of food to one another and gifts to the poor.***

Although Purim is not one of the Appointed Times of God, it is a great celebration of what God has done in our lives. The Pesach

(Passover) Seder reminds us that in every generation, there are those who rise up to destroy us, but our God saves us from their hand. In the time of the Book of Esther, Haman was the one who tried to destroy the Jewish people. In modern times, there have been those figures who have threatened the Jewish people, and there are echoes of Purim in their stories.

It is customary to hold carnival-like celebrations on Purim, to perform plays and parodies, and to hold costume contests. I have heard that the usual prohibitions against cross-dressing are lifted during this holiday, but I am not certain about that. Americans sometimes refer to Purim as the Jewish Mardi Gras.

Chanukah: Chanukah (transliterated hawn-u-kaw) is another self-imposed celebration of the Jewish people. Chanukah is probably one of the best known Jewish holidays, not because of any great religious significance, but because of its proximity to Christmas. Many non-Jews think of this holiday as the Jewish Christmas, as it has many Christmas customs, such as elaborate gift-giving, special music and decoration.

It is ironic that this holiday, which has its roots in a revolution against assimilation and the suppression of Jewish religion, has become the most assimilated, secular holiday on the Jewish calendar. However, it does have significant importance in Christian Scripture: ***22 "At that time the Feast of the Dedication took place at Jerusalem; 23 it was winter, and Jesus was walking in the temple in the portico of Solomon."*** (John 10:22-23)

Hmm, what does that Scripture have to do with Chanukah? Well you see the English word 'Dedication' is the Hebrew word Chanukah. So one must ask: if Jesus went up to Jerusalem for the Feast of Dedication, why don't followers of Jesus celebrate this Festival? Just say'n.

Beginning on the 25th of Kislev are the eight days of Chanukah... these were appointed a Festival with prayers of praise and thanksgiving. (Shabbat 21b, Babylonian Talmud) Chanukah, the festival of rededication, is also known as the festival of lights. A special nine candle Menorah is displayed in the windows of Jewish homes, and each night the candles are lit, illuminating the night. On the first night, the Shamish (transliterated shaw-mish and means servant) candle is lit and is used to light the first candle. Each successive night a candle is added until on the last night of Chanukah, all nine candles are burning brightly into the dark of night, for the entire neighborhood to see.

Chapter 11: What about Christmas and Easter?

As you probably know, neither Christmas nor Easter are mentioned in the Bible (at least in the original texts), because neither were initiated until far after, after the time of Jesus and/or the Disciples. Is it wrong to celebrate Christmas and Easter? No, indeed it is not!

Among the earliest Christians, no attempt was made to celebrate Jesus' birthday. According to history, it was not until 336 A.D. that the church in Rome fixed the date on December 25 and added Christmas Day to the list of officially recognized feast days. Although this was an edict of the Emperor, a few years later Pope Julius I made December 25th the official day of celebration of the birth of Jesus, for the church.

Saturnalia was an ancient Roman festival in honor of the deity Saturn, held on the 17th of December of the Julian calendar and later expanded with festivities to the 23rd of December. The holiday was celebrated with a sacrifice at the Temple of Saturn, in the Roman Forum, and a public banquet, followed by private gift-giving, continual partying, and a carnival atmosphere that overturned norms: gambling was permitted, and masters provided table service for their slaves. The poet Catullus called it "the best of days".

Why was December 25th chosen? There are many different traditions and theories as to why Christmas is celebrated on December 25th. A very early Christian tradition said that the day Mary was told she would have a very special baby, Jesus (called the Annunciation) was on March 25th - and it's still celebrated today on that date. Nine months after the 25th of March is the 25th of December! March 25th was also the day some early Christians thought the world had been made, and also the day that Jesus died.

December 25th might have also been chosen because the Winter Solstice and the ancient pagan Roman midwinter festivals, the aforementioned 'Saturnalia' and 'Dies Natalis Solis Invicti' took place in December around this date - so it was a time when people already celebrated things.

One final tradition is that Constantine wanted a Christian celebration that would be a counter action to the December pagan celebrations.

Should we, as many think, not celebrate Christmas because it has its roots in paganism? Well, if we take that posture then we must also eliminate birthdays, anniversaries, memorial services and many other modern day celebrations because they all have roots in paganism. Our worship services didn't start out as Christian or Jewish times of worship; their concept came from the worship of pagan gods of the Bedouins and other desert cultures.

What about the fact that God never told the people to celebrate Christmas? Again, he never told us to observe many things that we celebrate today. In fact two of the most famous and known celebrations of Judaism, Chanukah and the Feast of Esther, were *not* commanded by God, as pointed out earlier, but adopted by the people to celebrate specific times of freedom and the successful defeat of enemies who would have the destruction of God's people.

So here comes Christmas with it colorful lights, decorated trees, music, gifts and nativity displays; what's wrong with all of that? Nothing at all, as long as you (as they say) remember the 'reason for the season'. It is a celebration of the birth of Jesus; that seems like an excellent time to celebrate with food and festivities.

Easter, like Christmas, is another celebration imposed by mankind, rather than a commanded event from the Bible. Easter, which celebrates Jesus' resurrection from the dead, is Christianity's most important holiday. It has been called a moveable feast because it doesn't fall on a set date every year, as most holidays do. Instead, Christian churches in the West celebrate Easter on the first Sunday following the full moon after the vernal equinox on March 21. Therefore, Easter is observed anywhere between March 22 and April 25 every year. Orthodox Christians use the Julian calendar to calculate when Easter will occur and typically celebrate the holiday a week or two after the Western churches, which follow the Gregorian calendar.

There is some evidence that Christians originally celebrated the resurrection of Christ every Sunday, with observances such as Scripture readings, psalms, the Eucharist, and a prohibition against kneeling in prayer. At some point in the first two centuries, however, it became customary to celebrate the resurrection on one special day each year. Many of the religious observances of this celebration were taken from the Jewish Passover.

The specific day on which the resurrection should be celebrated became a major point of discussion, and at times controversy, within the early church. First, should it be on Jewish Passover no matter what day that falls, or should it always fall on a Sunday? It seems Christians in Asia took the former position, while those everywhere else insisted on the latter. The eminent church fathers Irenaeus and Polycarp were among the Asiatic Christians, and they claimed the authority of John the Apostle for their position. Nevertheless, the church majority officially decided that Easter should always be celebrated on a Sunday.

Chapter 12: Will You RSVP?

So now you know. The God of the Universe has invited you to have fellowship with Him, share a wonderful meal and immerse yourself in His Grace and Peace (Chesed v' Shalom). Not only are you invited once a week, but several times during the year.

I've asked this question before: what would you do, if the Governor of your State invited you to dinner? Would you go? Most of us would; we would get our hair cut or styled, maybe even buy a new set of clothes to wear. Men would polish their shoes and women would find the most complementary jewelry to wear. Now what if the President of the United States invited you to dinner; he's certainly bigger than the Governor! Even if we are of a different political or philosophical position than the Governor or President, I expect that most of us would still accept their invitation to dinner with excitement and zeal. So why wouldn't we do the same when the God of the Universe invites us to dinner? Is your answer different now? Are you going to accept God's invitations to dinner?

The Governor and President would expect us to RSVP (French: *répondez s'il vous plaît*) – *please let me know if you will be there.* This is usually accomplished by a phone call or note (these days often by email).

For thousands of years, God has been issuing invitations to dinner with Him. We can RSVP by committing ourselves to attend. Making the commitment, becoming excited about the event, putting on our finest clothes and saying "yes, I will attend". Nothing more and nothing less. Each time you accept one of God's invitations, you will be blessed. The more you accept, the more you will be blessed.

As I read and re-read Scripture, I discover the love and grace of our God. His desire for fellowship with His people is paramount in all that I read. The joy we receive from that fellowship, as the praise chorus says "is turned back in praise". Once again, let me say: The God of the Universe has invited *you* to dinner; will you go? Please RSVP.

Made in the USA
San Bernardino, CA
26 June 2018